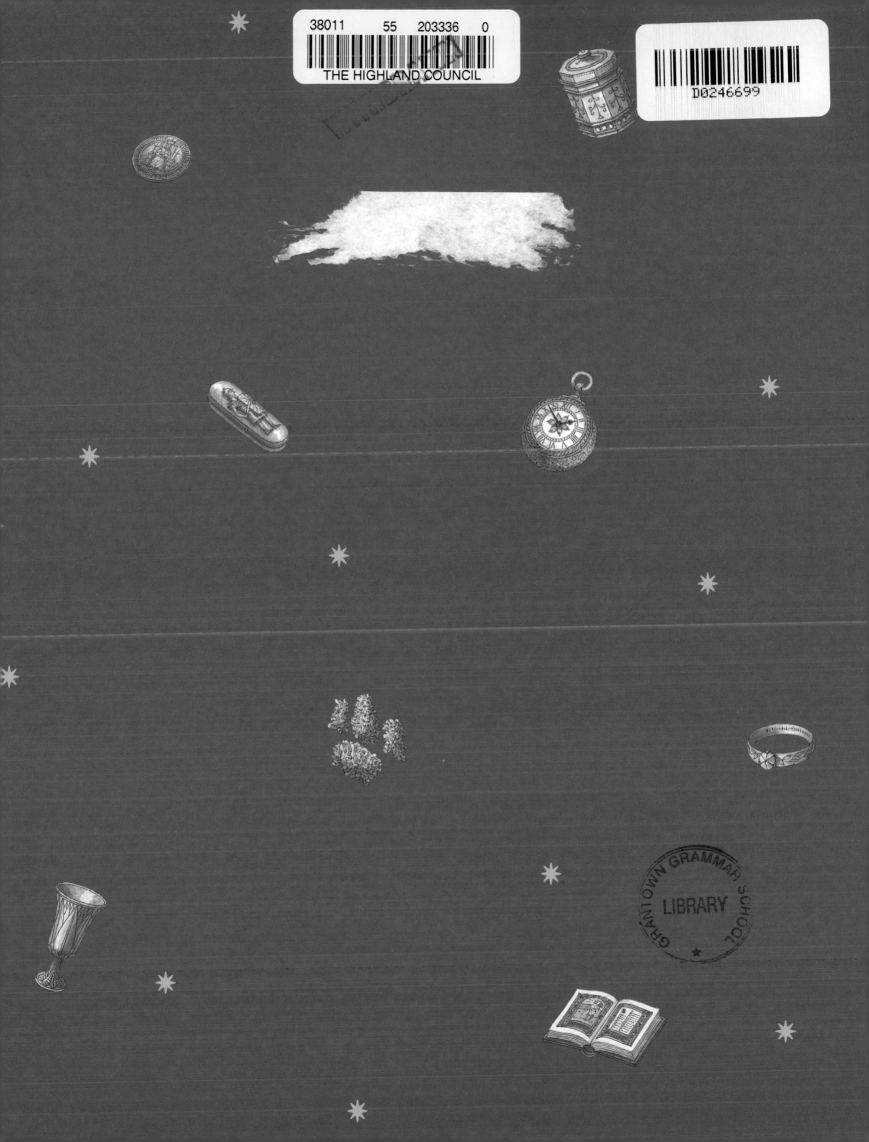

Gold

a treasure hunt through time

To Jill
M.H.

To my son, Richard
S.B.

Many thanks to:

Professor Martin Millet
Dr Richard Parkinson
Dr Joanna Story

Gold

a treasure hunt through time

Illustrated by
Stephen Biesty

✳

Written by
Meredith Hooper

Hodder
Children's
Books

A division of Hodder Headline Limited

Far off in distant space, massive stars explode in a brilliant, violent flash. The stars' outer layers are blown away by the incredible force of the explosions. They speed spectacularly out through the galaxy, carrying new elements created by the collapse.

In the centre of a vast cloud of rocks and dirty snowflakes, hydrogen and helium, gases begin to burn, forming a new star. Dust and rock pieces revolving round and round the new star start to clump together. Some form great solid balls. They are planets. One of them is our planet, Earth.

Hidden in Earth's crust are tiny amounts of a bright, shiny metal. The metal is soft yet strong. It docs not rust or decay. Always it gleams and glitters.

'I'he metal has travelled through space from the exploded stars.

It is gold.

G old gleams in narrow seams and veins deep underground. Sometimes the rocks carrying the gold jut above the surface, weathering in heat and frost. Pieces of gold fall out of the seams like seeds from a pod. Solid as beetles, thin as twisted threads.

Storms sweep the scraps of gold into rivers. They sink down through the water and collect on the river bed.

Beyond the boundaries of Egypt, out in the empty desert, sweating men search for gold. They sift through gravel in the beds of ancient rivers for grains of gold. They hunt in the crevices between boulders for water-worn nuggets.

The gold is packed in small linen bags and carried along dangerous routes back into Egypt to King Menkheperre in his royal palace.

A master goldsmith melts the gold and beats it into a smooth, glowing image of the King, a delicately beautiful mummy mask. The eyes stare out, inlaid with quartz and obsidian.

The mask will be placed on the King's mummy after he dies, so that his likeness will continue in the afterlife. The master goldsmith engraves a spell on the smooth inside of the mask, to protect Menkheperre from the dangers of the Underworld.

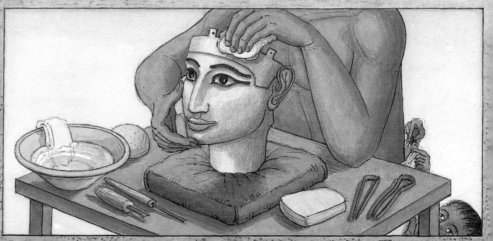

The King is dead. His embalmed body is laid in its cedar coffin. The priests fit the golden mask, heavy now with head-dress, collar and divine beard, over the mummy's head and shoulders. The coffin is placed inside another coffin, and another.

The huge funeral procession winds along the dusty valley towards the royal tomb tunnelled deep into the cliffs. Its entrance, high in a narrow cleft, is hidden in shadow.

The priests carry Menkheperre in his coffins out of the sunlight into a narrow passage which burrows steeply into the darkness. They take him down stairways and passages, snaking inside the silent rock.

They pass through the pillared antechamber to the furthest, deepest room. The burial chamber.

The coffins are lowered into the great stone sarcophagus. The heavy cover thuds shut and the king's mummy is sealed inside.

The final pictures and funeral texts are painted on the plastered walls. A single candle left burning gutters out. The priests block the entrances with stones, fill the outer passage with rubble.

Menkheperre will lie for all eternity inside his royal tomb.

The night is warm. The stars are sharp in the sky.

Men come creeping over the hills. They slither down the sides of the rocky cleft, break through the tomb entrance, squeeze down the rubble-filled corridor, feel for the steep, uneven stairs in the hot, airless dark. Stop on the edge of a deep pit. A thick rope snakes down into blackness. Then they are scaling the other side, breaking through the wall and into the antechamber heaped with the King's possessions.

But they want only one thing - the precious gold buried with the King. They search the floor, lever up the stones covering the secret stairs, and stumble down into the silent burial chamber.

In the flickering light from their oil lamps, they find the great sarcophagus. They force up the heavy cover. Tear off the lid of the first coffin, then the second. Quickly - quickly - throw the third aside. And there is the prize. The golden mask glitters below the black funeral pall. The smell of oils and resins drenching the King's mummy almost overpowers them.

They wrench off the mask, breaking it into pieces.
Now it's easier to carry.

Suddenly, heart-chilling calls of warning echo from men
keeping watch in the passages, from the look-outs on the cliff.
The punishments for tomb robbing are unrelenting.

They flee, dropping everything in their haste except the
golden mask that covered Menkheperre's face.
Professional robbers, desecrating the tomb of the King.

The mummy mask must be turned into something new.
Fast. The thieves sell the gold. It is beaten into a tall,
elegant lotus chalice and given by a king and queen as
a gift to a temple. There, year after year, priests use it
in the temple services.

In Rome, the Emperor Nero is young. And extremely rich.
He wants the best and most beautiful things in the world
for his new palace.

At the great temple in far-off Egypt, Nero's officials arrive, collecting
treasures. The priests walk with slow, reluctant steps to the back of the
temple, where crypts are hidden in the thickness of the wall.
The priests unlock the door. They take the golden lotus chalice,
used for more than a thousand years of temple services,
and give it to the officials.

In Rome, Nero transforms the city into pretend country.
From his palace windows he can see wild animals running
through woods, and watch the birds swoop over an artifical lake.
He gives a sumptuous dinner party. His guests eat from his
newly gathered golden treasures.

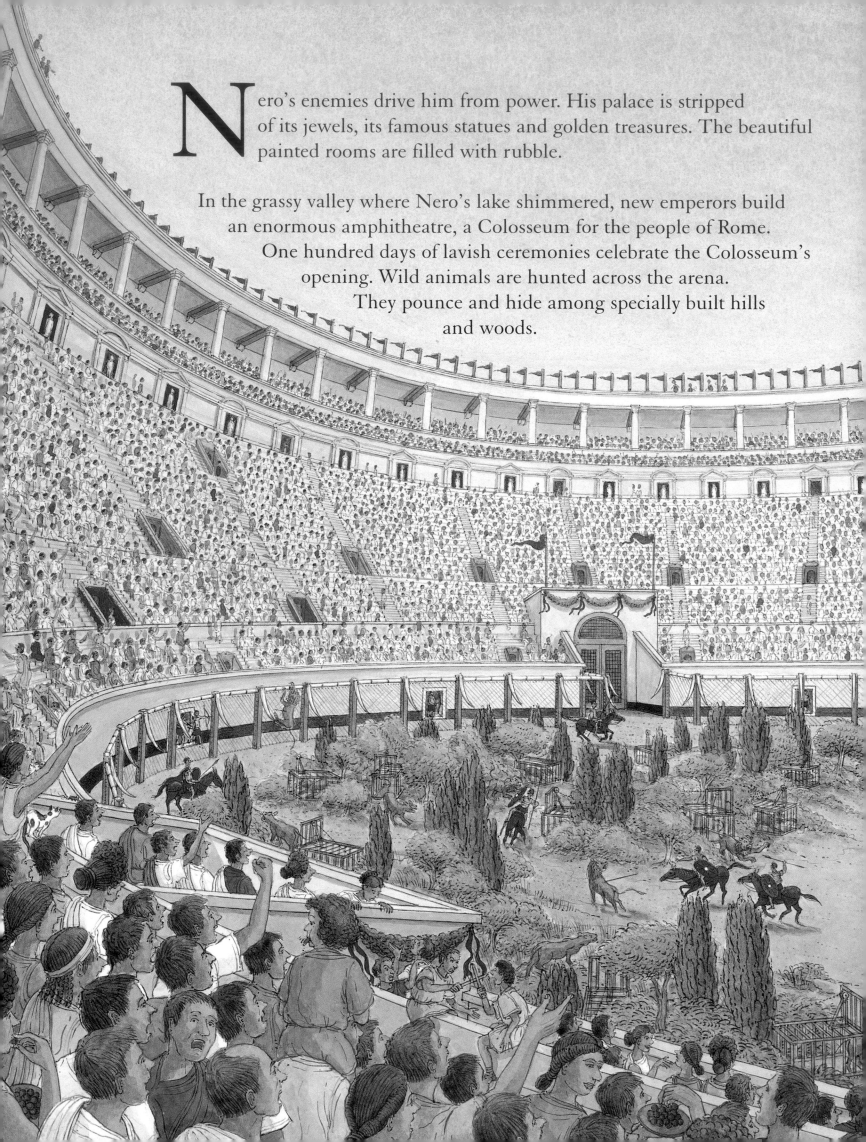

Nero's enemies drive him from power. His palace is stripped of its jewels, its famous statues and golden treasures. The beautiful painted rooms are filled with rubble.

In the grassy valley where Nero's lake shimmered, new emperors build an enormous amphitheatre, a Colosseum for the people of Rome. One hundred days of lavish ceremonies celebrate the Colosseum's opening. Wild animals are hunted across the arena. They pounce and hide among specially built hills and woods.

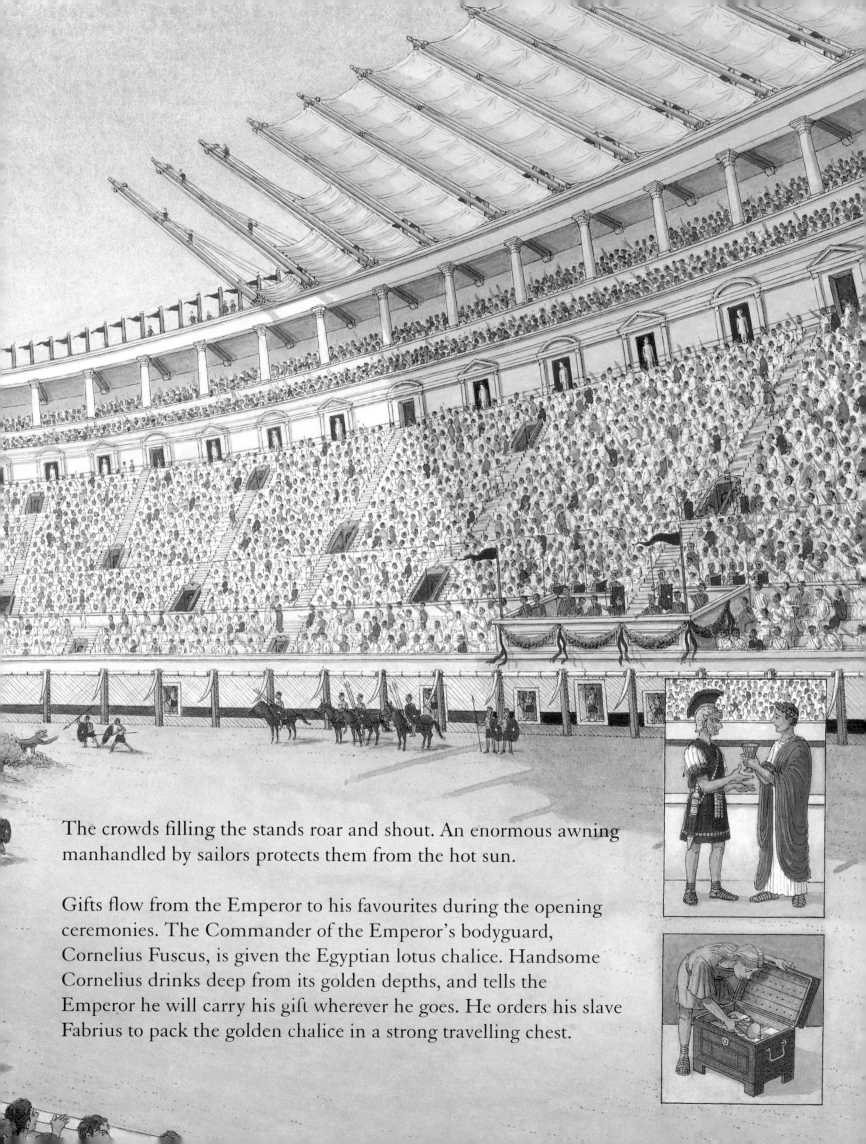

The crowds filling the stands roar and shout. An enormous awning manhandled by sailors protects them from the hot sun.

Gifts flow from the Emperor to his favourites during the opening ceremonies. The Commander of the Emperor's bodyguard, Cornelius Fuscus, is given the Egyptian lotus chalice. Handsome Cornelius drinks deep from its golden depths, and tells the Emperor he will carry his gift wherever he goes. He orders his slave Fabrius to pack the golden chalice in a strong travelling chest.

Cornelius Fuscus is appointed commander of an expeditionary army. He marches with his soldiers north, then east. He marches beyond the boundary of the Roman Empire, crossing the wide river Danube.

The Roman army enters the land of the Dacians. Without warning, the Dacians attack. Cornelius Fuscus is killed. Decebalus the King swoops on the baggage train, his men hurling spears and slashing with large, curved swords. Looting. Slaying. Triumphant. The Romans are beaten.

Fabrius the slave manages to break into his master's travelling chest and grab the golden chalice. He flees from the battle, the yelling and turmoil, the confusion, panic and slaughter. He rubs mud into his hair, dirties his face, rips his clothes, so no one will recognise him. Fabrius runs, hungry, frightened, along the banks of the great river.

His golden treasure is quickly stolen. It passes from thief to thief. West of the land of the Dacians, a horse-riding warrior king seizes the rich and strange booty. He locks it in the treasure room of his palace with other precious gold. Proof of royal power and strength, as son succeeds father, generation after generation.

T he armies of the great
King Charlemagne sweep east across
Europe, conquering, burning, capturing slaves.

Charlemagne's armies reach the palace of the warrior kings.
His men break open the treasure room. Their astonished eyes
see vast heaps of glittering gold and silver, fabulous jewels,
brilliant silks.

The treasure is packed into fifteen strong wooden carts, each pulled by four
oxen. The oxen heave across forested mountains, green pastures, taking the
treasure back to King Charlemagne. Just after crossing a river one of the carts
hits a boulder as it creaks up a hill. It jolts heavily. Bowls and caskets tumble out.

No one notices the lotus chalice lying half buried in the leaves. A slender, beautiful chalice, made before imagining in far-away Egypt from stolen gold. Now a mouse hides inside. Spiders spin webs across its smooth curves.

Saplings sprout in the ox carts' tracks. The trunks thicken and grow tall. Every autumn, pigs snuffle through the woods for acorns. Every winter, wolves pad across the snow which covers the earth where the golden chalice lies hidden.

The forest spreads. Trees age, then
rot and topple. Young trees jostle
to fill the spaces.

Woodcutters go into the forest searching
for straight thick trunks. They need timber
for the castle they are building above
the river.

More trees are cleared to make space for fields.
Now the brown earth lies exposed to hard frost
and drying sun.

One spring, as a peasant ploughs, he sees
something glinting among the clods. He bends
down, shakes the thing free of mud, spits on it,
rubs it with his sleeve. In his hands is a strange
long cup. Battered. Bent. With no base.
But heavy. The heaviness of gold!
Buried treasure!

The Lord of the castle knows everything that happens. He sends his Steward to seize the cup.

The Steward climbs the tower to the castle strongroom. Here the Lord keeps his treasure chest, in a niche in the wall. He unlocks the wrought-iron gates. His master does not care what the battered cup is, or might have been. It's gold. That's all that matters.

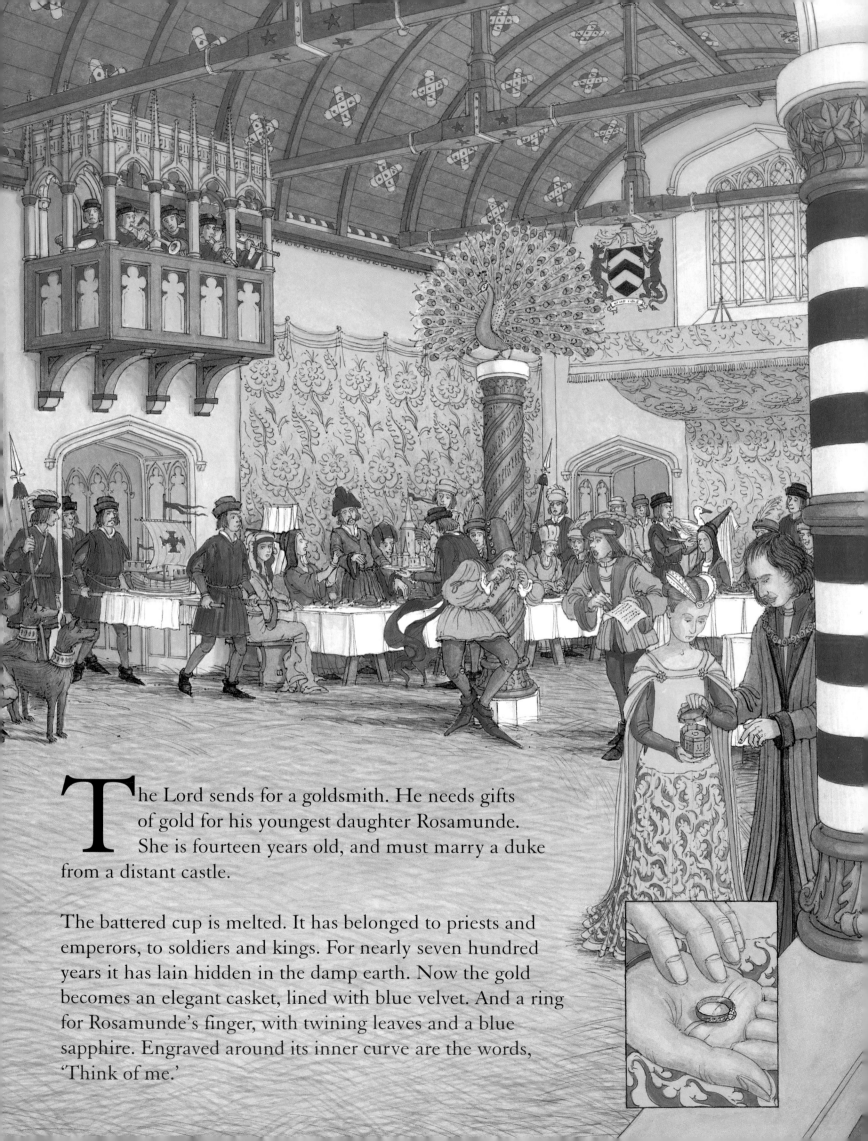

The Lord sends for a goldsmith. He needs gifts of gold for his youngest daughter Rosamunde. She is fourteen years old, and must marry a duke from a distant castle.

The battered cup is melted. It has belonged to priests and emperors, to soldiers and kings. For nearly seven hundred years it has lain hidden in the damp earth. Now the gold becomes an elegant casket, lined with blue velvet. And a ring for Rosamunde's finger, with twining leaves and a blue sapphire. Engraved around its inner curve are the words, 'Think of me.'

Rosamunde's wedding is celebrated with a great feast.
There are ships and castles made out of sugar, and
live birds fly out of a pie. In the castle courtyard a
grand tournament is held, with knights jousting in
shining armour.

But a small part of the lotus chalice remains.
In the fall from Charlemagne's treasure cart, the
foot bent. Deep in the earth the foot snapped off,
and still lies hidden.

The goldsmith keeps the thin shavings and tiny scraps of gold left over from making the casket and ring. They are his by right. He sells them to an artist in the splendid city of Bruges.

Gerard the artist grinds the gold to a fine powder, mixing it with a liquid made by boiling animal skins. Carefully he pours the mixture into a little pot. He puts on his silk painting clothes and cap. No dust or hairs can drop on his delicate paintings.

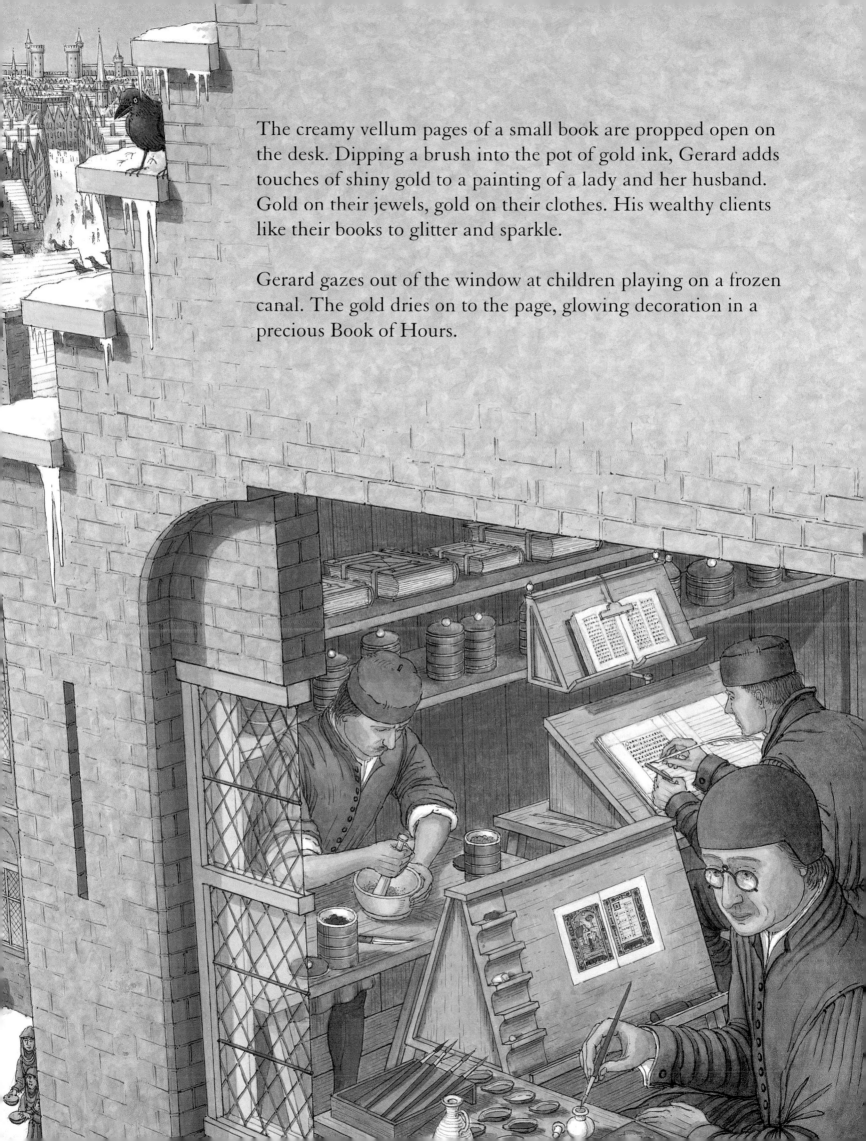

The creamy vellum pages of a small book are propped open on the desk. Dipping a brush into the pot of gold ink, Gerard adds touches of shiny gold to a painting of a lady and her husband. Gold on their jewels, gold on their clothes. His wealthy clients like their books to glitter and sparkle.

Gerard gazes out of the window at children playing on a frozen canal. The gold dries on to the page, glowing decoration in a precious Book of Hours.

Queen Elizabeth of England isn't taking enough notice of Ambassador Adolphus. Adolphus is trying to compete with eleven other foreign ambassadors, all hoping to persuade the Queen to marry their masters. Elizabeth jokes, and teases, and keeps them all waiting.

Now everyone is staying at the palace of an English Earl. The Queen is being entertained with music, banquets, dancing and hunting. The Earl wants to marry her as well.

But Ambassador Adolphus has a plan. The Queen's maid-of-honour Katherine has promised to talk to the Queen, and tell her about his master, the Duke.

Katherine will tell the Queen how handsome and tall the Duke is, how fond he is of hunting, what a good husband he will make.

Adolphus looks at a chest of presents chosen from the treasure room of his master's castle. He picks out an elegant gold casket, then sidles up to Katherine.

Katherine opens the casket. Inside is a gold ring with twining leaves set with a blue sapphire. Katherine holds up the ring. 'Think of me,' she reads, and smiles. Ambassador Adolphus glows with hope. Surely tonight the Queen will hear his master praised.

Katherine puts the gold ring on her finger, and asks her brother to look after the gold casket. But before he can lock it away he is robbed. Slippery as grease, the gold casket passes between thieves in London's crowded streets.

The river races roaring under London Bridge, brown scum frothing into dirty foam. Carts rumble along the narrow roadway between the buildings. A man squeezes up against a shop-front, then slips through a door into a goldsmith's workshop. In minutes the casket that once belonged to Rosamunde is melting in the fierce heat of the goldsmith's furnace. All proof of the robbery disappears into shimmering liquid gold.

In a hidden room, up narrow stairs, a forger works in secret. If he's caught he'll hang. He takes gold from the casket and plates the surfaces of false coins made from cheap metal. The counterfeit coins gleam like true gold sovereigns.

Down below, the goldsmith makes a fine watch-case from the rest of the casket gold. A rich student buys the watch. But in winter's cold he leaves it in an Oxford tavern, and the tavern-keeper sells it.

Katherine hides her golden ring, and forgets where.

The counterfeit coins are passed to the Captain of a ship, the Dragon, moored by London Bridge. The Captain locks the money in a small iron-bound chest.

'A sail! A sail!' The Dragon gives chase. The Spanish merchant ship is slow, laden with goods. The Dragon draws closer, cannons firing. Then grapples the merchant ship. Soldiers leap aboard gripping pikes and swords.

The Spaniards fight hard, defending their ship. But they are defeated.

The cargo is valuable - wine and oil, spices, sugar, silks and carpets, china dishes, a bag of pearls. The Captain of the Dragon sends the defeated ship back to England as his prize. Queen Elizabeth will take a share of the plunder, and so will the government. But there is enough to make the Captain and his crew wealthy.

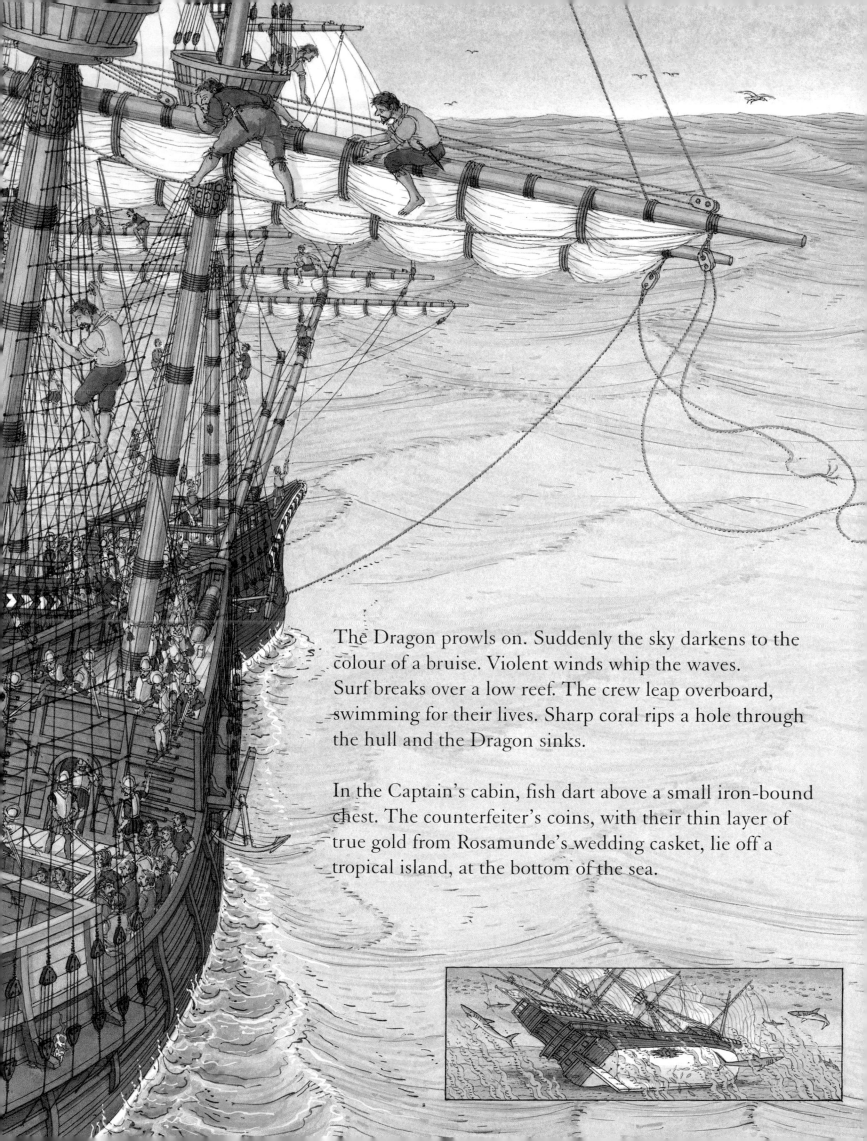

The Dragon prowls on. Suddenly the sky darkens to the colour of a bruise. Violent winds whip the waves. Surf breaks over a low reef. The crew leap overboard, swimming for their lives. Sharp coral rips a hole through the hull and the Dragon sinks.

In the Captain's cabin, fish dart above a small iron-bound chest. The counterfeiter's coins, with their thin layer of true gold from Rosamunde's wedding casket, lie off a tropical island, at the bottom of the sea.

An old gold watch hangs by a thread
inside a large glass globe, ticking clearly. Robert Boyle
is showing visitors his laboratory in Oxford.

'And now for the experiment,' says Boyle. His assistant begins pumping
the air out of the glass globe. The watch's tick gets fainter... and fainter...
until no more air can be pumped out. The visitors press their ears to
the glass. No ticking can be heard at all. But the watch's hands
are still moving.

Gradually the air is allowed back into the glass globe. The tick sounds again,
louder and louder.

'And that, gentlemen,' says the Honourable Robert Boyle, 'seems to prove that
air is needed to carry sound.'

Mr Sadler, an Oxford shopkeeper, inflates his magnificent balloon with hydrogen gas. Underneath hangs a boat-shaped carriage equipped with wings and oars. Mr Sadler wants to be the first Englishman to fly. Once up in the sky, he plans to do experiments with air.

Mr Sadler climbs into the carriage. The ropes are released. The balloon shoots up, rising at great speed. Immense, excited crowds watch, heads craning, astonished.

A young scientist holds a heavy old-fashioned gold watch. 'A man has flown for three minutes! Unbelievable!'

High in the sky the balloon lurches on out of sight.

The young scientist travels to Paris. He sells his heavy old watch to a goldsmith and uses the money to enjoy himself. There's so much to do in Paris!

The goldsmith makes exquisite things for fashionable people. The gold from the watch-case becomes a small, elegant toothpick holder, with a Roman soldier engraved on the lid, and a mirror inside.

A royal tax-gatherer buys the toothpick holder. He travels to the palace of Versailles to speak to the King.

Versailles is crowded with courtiers, noblemen and beautiful ladies. His new toothpick holder is admired. 'I want it!' says a Countess. 'Of course,' says the tax-gatherer. 'But I admire your fan.' 'You may have it,' says the Countess.

At that moment King Louis XV1 and Queen
Marie-Antoinette enter. Versailles is magnificent.
The King is magnificent. Nothing will ever change.

But everything does change. Revolution and war sweep
through France and Europe. The Countess, in great danger,
gives the golden toothpick holder to a young English army officer
who saves her life.

Back home, the officer turns the toothpick holder into five
fine gold buttons for his waistcoat. He tells everybody who
admires the gleaming buttons how he saved a
French Countess.

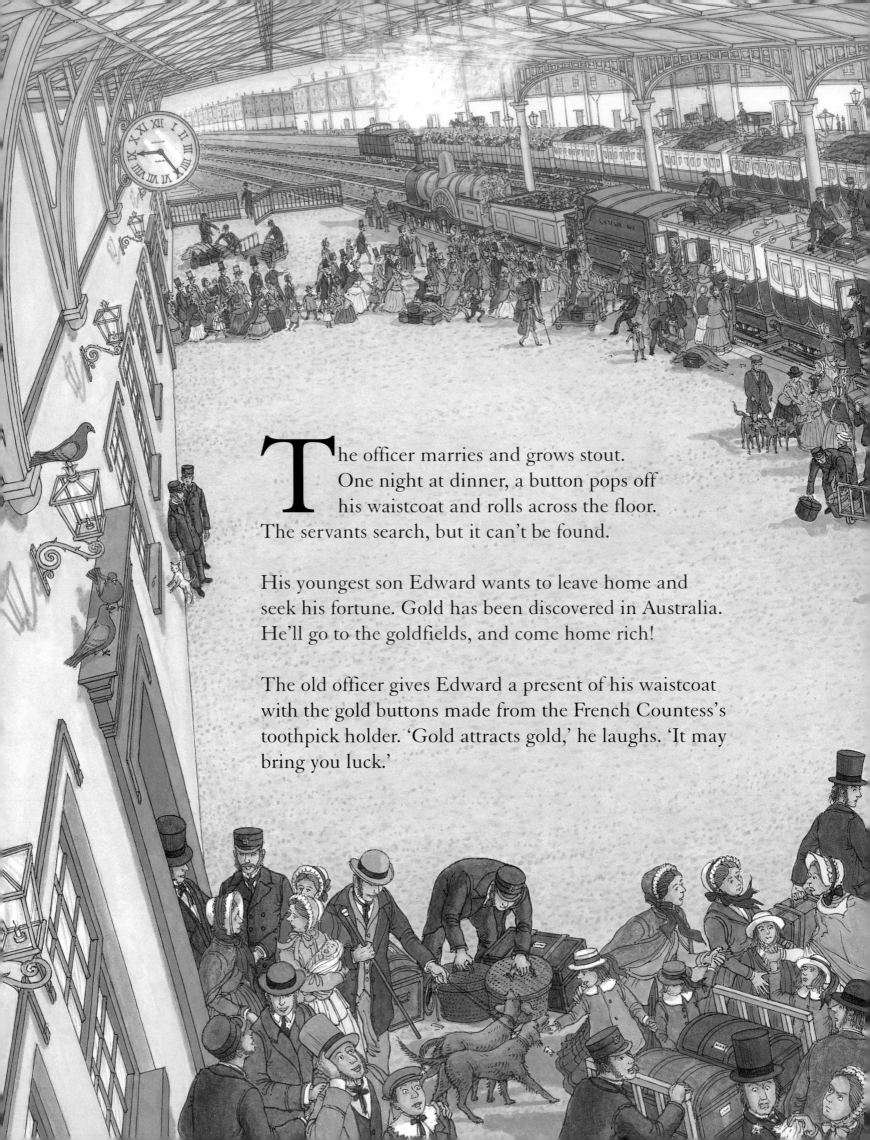

The officer marries and grows stout.
One night at dinner, a button pops off
his waistcoat and rolls across the floor.
The servants search, but it can't be found.

His youngest son Edward wants to leave home and
seek his fortune. Gold has been discovered in Australia.
He'll go to the goldfields, and come home rich!

The old officer gives Edward a present of his waistcoat
with the gold buttons made from the French Countess's
toothpick holder. 'Gold attracts gold,' he laughs. 'It may
bring you luck.'

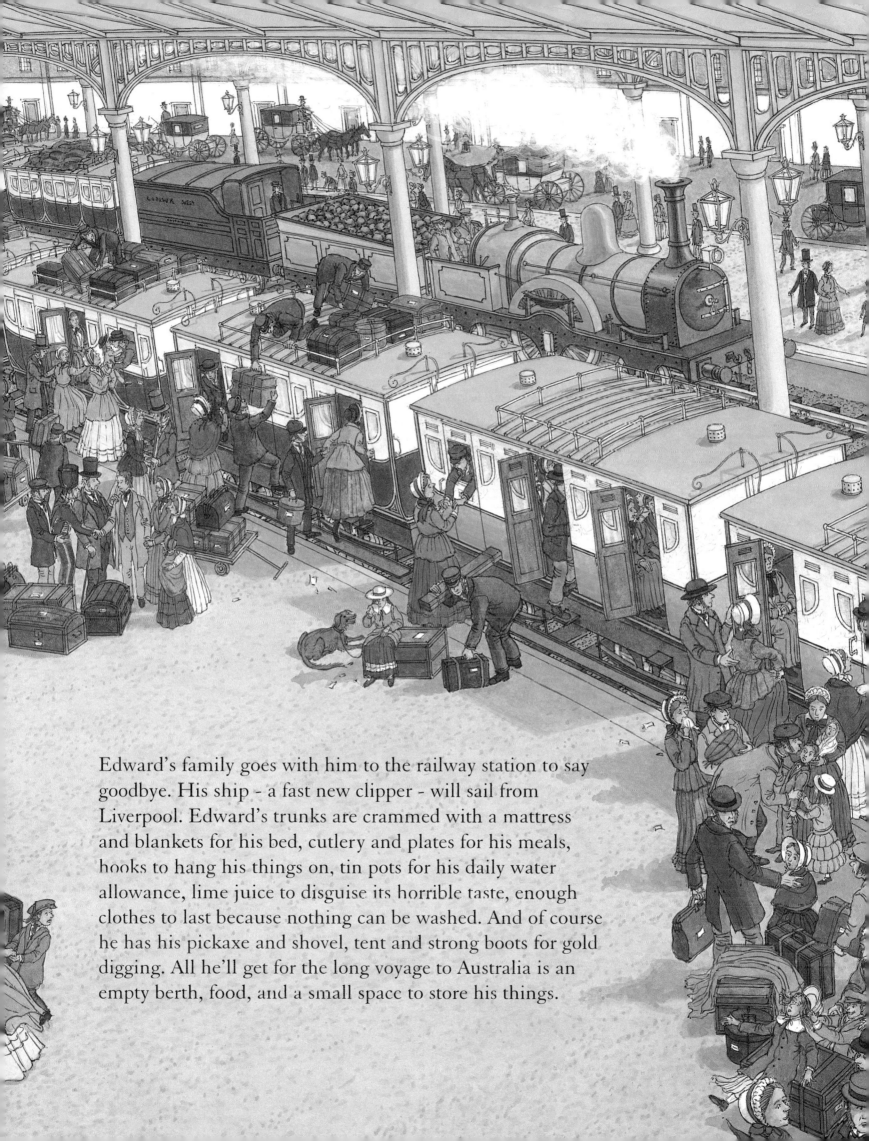

Edward's family goes with him to the railway station to say goodbye. His ship - a fast new clipper - will sail from Liverpool. Edward's trunks are crammed with a mattress and blankets for his bed, cutlery and plates for his meals, hooks to hang his things on, tin pots for his daily water allowance, lime juice to disguise its horrible taste, enough clothes to last because nothing can be washed. And of course he has his pickaxe and shovel, tent and strong boots for gold digging. All he'll get for the long voyage to Australia is an empty berth, food, and a small space to store his things.

The ship is crowded with 725 emigrants. But Edward is happy. He likes being at sea. On hot nights he sleeps on the deck, and washes his face at dawn in a bucket of salty water. He helps the sailors hauling at the ropes.

Then they are far to the south, racing through magnificent mountainous waves. The sails strain in the shrieking winds. The ship rolls and lurches. Meals slide across the tables, precious possessions tumble and break, babies cry, their mothers are weak with seasickness. Then icebergs loom, white islands of rock-hard ice. People wail with fear, and shiver in the sleet and unexpected cold. But Edward and other young men have a snowball fight.

Edward notices a pretty young woman, secretly looking at him.
He tells her the story of his golden waistcoat buttons; and by the end
of the long voyage they agree to get married. So the golden buttons
bring him luck, after all.

The spicy scent of land wafts towards them. They see huge cliffs,
sandy beaches, strange grey-green trees. Australia at last. It's the first
land for 73 days.

Everybody is gold-mad. Edward has no luck at the diggings, so he
finds a job driving a flock of two thousand sheep across country. But
his new wife Louisa has a brother in San Francisco. She persuades
Edward to travel to America.

In San Francisco Edward begins writing for a newspaper. He and
Louisa build a wooden house, settle down, and have seven children.

Carefully, Louisa folds Edward's father's waistcoat with the golden buttons and puts it in a trunk. She adds his mother's letters, tied in a ribbon. America is now their home.

The trunk travels from house to house across America, battered, somehow never thrown away.

One Christmas the great great great granddaughter of Edward and Louisa climbs to the attic of her grandparents' house. She pokes around in the dusty cold looking at favourite toys and faded photographs, broken chairs and an old typewriter. In a corner she finds the battered trunk, and unfolds the moth-eaten waistcoat.

She snips off one of the shiny buttons, and takes it back to New York. A friend turns it into a necklace. She walks along New York's streets, feeling happy, the golden button glinting in the sun.

A button which came from a set of waistcoat buttons, which were made from the gold of a toothpick holder; which came from a gold watch-case, which was part of a golden marriage casket; which was made out of gold from a lotus chalice; which came from a golden mummy mask, covering the face of a dead king.

Three and a half thousand years ago.
In ancient Egypt.

Where is the gold from the mummy mask now?

The broken foot from the Egyptian chalice is still buried in the ground, near the west bank of the river Rhine. Grapevines push their roots down past its ancient curves.

The illuminated book made in Bruges is a precious Book of Hours in a library.

The gold ring was found behind wooden panelling when alterations were made to the room where Katherine hid it. Now it is in a display case in a museum.

The counterfeit gold coins lie on the sea bed off Jamaica, under layers of soft silt.

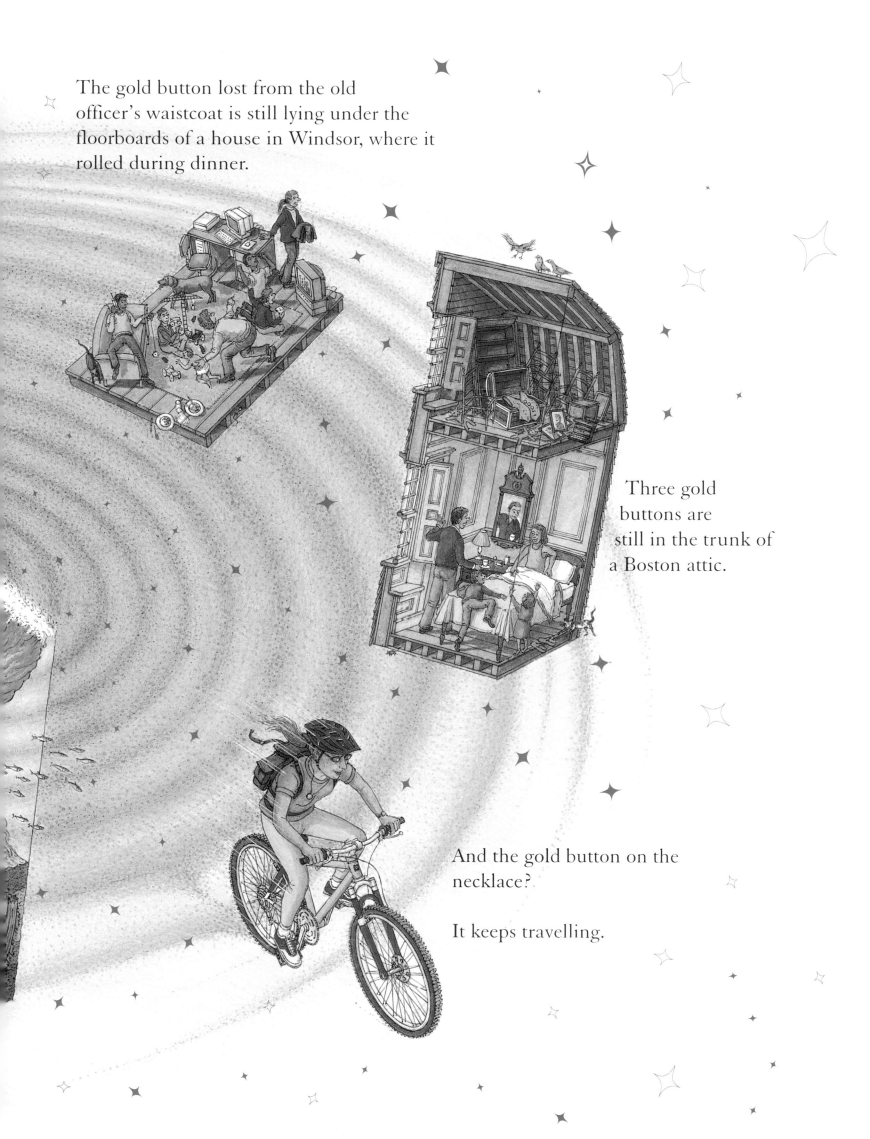

The gold button lost from the old officer's waistcoat is still lying under the floorboards of a house in Windsor, where it rolled during dinner.

Three gold buttons are still in the trunk of a Boston attic.

And the gold button on the necklace?

It keeps travelling.

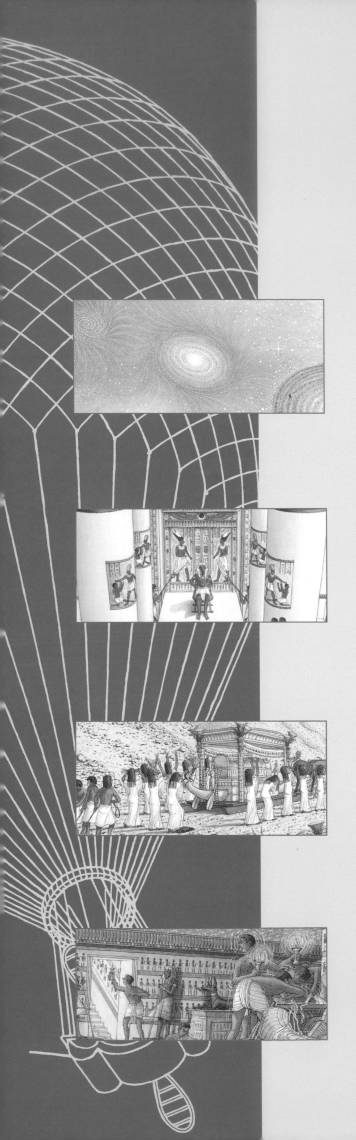

*M*uch of this story is based on real places and real events. Some of the people are invented, some real. But everything in this story could have happened . . .

The gold on Earth was created during the explosive deaths of massive stars called supernovae five billion years or more ago. Gold is a rare metal. In every two thousand tonnes of Earth's crust there is only enough gold to make one small ring.

The gold in the story was mined to the south of Egypt about 3500 years ago. The king is similar to Tuthmosis III who reigned from 1479 to 1425 BC. We can't be sure if Tuthmosis had a golden mummy mask because his tomb was robbed soon after his burial.

The tomb in the story is similar to the tomb of Tuthmosis III, which can be visited in the Valley of the Kings near Luxor, Egypt. A king's golden mummy mask, belonging to Tutankhamun, has survived and is in the Egyptian Museum, Cairo.

The tomb in the story was robbed about 1400 BC. Golden treasures like the lotus chalice were used in Egyptian temples as part of the services for a divine cult. An elegant lotus chalice made of blue faience is in the British Museum, London.

Nero became emperor of Rome at the age of 17 in AD 54. An Egyptian temple still stands at Dendera with hidden crypts, similar to the one in the story.

In the story, Nero's soldiers collected the lotus chalice along with other treasures in AD 63. Nero used the chalice the next year in the octagonal room of his newly built palace, Domus Aurea (the Golden House), in Rome. Domus Aurea has been excavated and is open to the public.

Nero was killed at the age of 30. The Emperor Titus celebrated the opening of the Colosseum in Rome in AD 80 with 100 days of events. Cornelius Fuscus was Commander of the Praetorian Guard. Favourites like Cornelius would have been given gifts during the celebrations. The Colosseum can be visited.

Cornelius Fuscus led an army of about 15,000 men over the Danube into Dacia (modern Romania) in AD 86. He was killed in battle. Carved scenes of the powerful Dacian King Decebalus and his army can be seen on Trajan's column in Rome. In the story, Fabrius the slave took the lotus chalice to Pannonia (modern Hungary), the province next to Dacia. The chalice would have been stored in the treasure room of the kings of the Avars.

Charlemagne the Great conquered the Avar Empire at the end of the eighth century. The palace of the kings, known as The Ring, was burnt around 796 and the treasure taken back to Charlemagne probably to his palace in Aachen. Charlemagne distributed the treasure widely, but very few pieces can be traced today.

Many treasures have been found hidden in the ground. Sometimes the treasure was buried for safety, especially during wars. Sometimes it was lost, or dropped. In the story, the chalice was dug up in 1465 in a field near a castle on the west bank of the Rhine, in modern Germany.

In the story, Rosamunde's wedding took place in 1468. The ring and casket would have travelled with her to her husband's castle. After her death it would have been kept in the castle treasure room. Rings similar to Rosamunde's can be seen in museums like the Victoria & Albert in London.

The city of Bruges (now in Belgium) was a famous centre for hand-made illuminated books. Examples from this time can be seen in libraries, museums and churches around the world. But there are still illuminated books lying undiscovered and unnoticed. In the story, Gerard the artist was painting the Book of Hours in 1480.

In August 1559, Queen Elizabeth I of England was 25 years old. She stayed for five days at Nonesuch Palace, being entertained by one of her suitors, the Earl of Arundel. Nonesuch Palace was destroyed late in the 17th century. In the story, the ring and casket came to England in a chest of treasures and gifts to be used as bribes by the ambassador of another of the Queen's suitors - a German Duke, descended from Rosamunde.

In the story, the counterfeit gold sovereigns and the gold watch-case were made in 1559. A typical counterfeiting technique was to use a core of base metal of the correct weight, and plate the surface with precious metal. London Bridge, with its crowded narrow roadway between high leaning houses, was the only bridge across the River Thames until the middle of the 18th century.

During England's war with Spain many English ships attacked enemy ships wherever they could find them. Wrecks lie scattered at the bottom of the sea. The coins in the story sank in the Spanish West Indies aboard an English privateer around 1586.

The air pump experiment was carried out in Oxford by the Honourable Robert Boyle and his assistant Robert Hooke in 1659. The site of Boyle's house is marked by a plaque on the wall of University College. Mr Sadler's balloon was launched late in 1784 and flew for some miles until it came down in a hedge. A plaque on the wall of Merton College commemorates the flight.

In the story, the old-fashioned watch-case was turned into a toothpick holder in Paris in 1785. The French Revolution began in 1789. The Palace of Versailles can be visited today.

The young English army officer saved the Countess in 1812 during the Napoleonic Wars, and returned home when the fighting ended in 1815.

Gold was discovered in California in 1848 and people rushed to the diggings from all over the world. Gold was discovered in Australia in 1851 and a new gold rush started. Half a million people arrived in Australia during the next ten years to try their luck.
In the story, Edward left home for the gold rushes in 1854, from Euston Station.

In the story, Edward sailed from the port of Liverpool to Melbourne, Australia on one of the fast new American-built clipper ships. The clippers travelled a new route dipping far to the south, and were famous record-breakers. Edward and Louisa left Australia in 1857, sailing across the Pacific Ocean to California.

In the story, Edward and Louisa's great great great granddaughter walks along Fifth Avenue past the Empire State Building in New York in spring, in the first year of the 21st century.

Glossary

Antechamber	*A small room leading to a main one.*
Chalice	*A drinking cup.*
Clipper	*A fast sailing ship.*
Counterfeit	*Fake, forged.*
Desecrating	*Treating with violent disrespect.*
Embalmed	*Preserved, often using scented spices.*
Faience	*Decorated earthenware.*
Hydrogen	*A gas.*
Helium	*A gas.*
Lotus	*A water lily.*
Obsidian	*A hard, dark, glassy rock.*
Quartz	*A hard mineral, often in the form of colourless or white crystals.*
Resin	*A sticky substance found in the sap of plants such as pine trees.*
Sarcophagus	*A stone coffin.*
Sovereign	*A gold coin.*
Suitor	*A man who seeks to marry a woman.*
Vellum	*Fine parchment made of calf's skin, used to write or draw on.*

Text copyright 2002 © Meredith Hooper
Illustration copyright 2002 © Stephen Biesty
Published by Hodder Children's Books 2002

The right of Meredith Hooper and Stephen Biesty to be identified as the
author and illustrator of the Work has been asserted by them in accordance
with the Copyright, Designs and Patents Act 1988.

Picture research by Linda Proud

Cover concept by Raymond Stoffel

10 9 8 7 6 5 4 3 2 1

A catalogue record for this book is available from the British Library.
Biesty, Stephen
Gold: a treasure hunt through time
1. Gold – Juvenile literature 2. Gold – History – Juvenile literature
I. Title II. Hooper, Meredith
669.2'2'09

ISBN 0 340 78855 0

Printed in Hong Kong by Wing King Tong

Hodder Children's Books
a division of Hodder Headline Limited
338 Euston Road
London NW1 3BH